I0667441

PRAYER FIRST AID KIT

PRAYER FIRST AID KIT

Summersdale Publishers Ltd
46 West Street
Chichester
West Sussex
PO19 1RP
UK

www.summersdale.com

Printed and bound in the Czech Republic

ISBN: 978-1-84953-734-6

Substantial discounts on bulk quantities of Summersdale books are available to corporations, professional associations and other organisations. For details contact Nicky Douglas by telephone: +44 (0) 1243 756902, fax: +44 (0) 1243 786300 or email: nicky@summersdale.com.

PRAYER FIRST AID KIT

Prayers for Everyday Dilemmas, Decisions and Emergencies

VICTORIA LORENZATO

summersdale

For Neil,
my compass in all of the storms of life,
especially the ones in a teacup!

CONTENTS

Introduction...8

Everyday Life...10

The Early Years..24

Matters of the Heart..............................40

Parenting and Family Life.....................56

For Our World in Need...........................74

Tackling Temptation...............................86

Caring for Mind and Body......................98

Providing...111

The Golden Years...................................125

Seeking Answers to the Big Questions......138

Praying Through the Year......................149

INTRODUCTION

In the same way that human relationships rely upon good communication, all major world faiths advocate the importance of prayer in strengthening a person's faith in addition to their relationship with God. Whether you have grown up in a religious family or not, whether you have vivid childhood memories of reciting prayers at school assemblies or in church, a regular prayer habit can have many personal benefits.

I have clear memories of a teacher explaining prayer to me as a child; reminding the class that prayer doesn't provide instant results or secret formulas for getting exactly what we ask for. Decades later, I can see that the true gift and beauty of prayer is the recognition that we are not alone and that by taking the time to pray before rushing impulsively into a situation or decision, we allow ourselves the opportunity to breathe and reflect first.

The intention of this book is to provide you with a selection of prayers that could be used in a variety of situations that you might find yourself in at the many different stages of your life. In moments of stress, it can be difficult to find the right words to express how you are feeling and these prayers offer you a starting point in your conversation with God. Keep in mind the benefit of listening as well as speaking.

At the heart of a person's faith is the recognition that we are part of something bigger than ourselves and for that reason there are also many prayers here for those moments when you want to pray for others; at times it can seem as though prayer is all that you have to offer.

I have included a selection of prayers written over the last 3,000 years, with the intention of alleviating any sense that you are the first and only person afflicted with your current difficulty; the challenges of living a good life seem to transcend any geographical, cultural or historical boundary. When asked whether I believe that prayer can really make a difference to our lives, I am reminded of the words of St Madeleine Sophie Barat:

> Make prayer your delight; there find your
> rest and your happiness.

Victoria Lorenzato, 2015

EVERYDAY LIFE

When I wake up

To begin your day with prayer is to clothe yourself in faith, ready for what lies ahead. The following is an excerpt from a fifth-century prayer attributed to St Patrick.

I bind unto myself today
The virtues of the starlit heaven,
The glorious sun's life-giving ray,
The whiteness of the moon at even,
The flashing of the lightning free,
The whirling wind's tempestuous shocks,
The stable earth, the deep salt sea,
Around the old eternal rocks.

I bind unto myself today
The power of God to hold and lead,
His eye to watch, His might to stay,
His ear to hearken to my need.
The wisdom of my God to teach,
His hand to guide, His shield to ward,
The word of God to give me speech,
His heavenly host to be my guard.

St Patrick (387–461 AD)

Before meals

A short prayer to recognise our need for spiritual as well as physical sustenance.

Lord,

As the meal before me physically sustains me, I thank you for the spiritual nourishment that you provide. Recognising that the world has enough resources to feed every family, I ask your blessing upon those who work to feed those who are hungry and I ask you to help me to be more aware of the needs of others.

Amen

When I am delayed

Combat the toxic mix of panic and impatience with this short prayer.

In moments like this, Lord,

I am reminded of the importance of seeking out your plan for me. As I wait to continue on my journey, I ask for the patience and wisdom to use this time constructively. What can I learn in this time? Who can I remember in prayer? I seek your help at this present moment in recalling the true value of time and what it means to spend it well.

Amen

God be in my heart,
and in my thinking;
God be at my end,
and at my departing.

The Sarum Primer

Feeling misunderstood

Sometimes our best intentions can have disastrous results and we can feel great frustration.

God,

Is it just me? I'm having one of those days where no one seems to understand me. It is easy to feel like giving up on some people! You have known me since before I was born; help me to take heart in that knowledge as I seek new ways to connect with others.

Amen

In gratitude

It's important to remember not only to pray when we need something; saying 'thank you' feels good.

I thank you, Lord,

For the many blessings that this day has brought to me. I know that all things are possible with faith in you and as I learn to see the plan that you have for my life, I seek the grace to accept with gratitude the many moments of joy that unfold each day. It can be easy to rush through the day and overlook these; help me to take greater notice of each one.

Amen

When all seems lost

The following reflection, which opens with an extract from Psalm 46, is a timely reminder of the importance of acknowledging God's presence in our lives.

'Be still and know that I am God,'
That I who made and gave thee life
Will lead thy faltering steps aright;
That I who see each sparrow's fall
Will hear and heed thy earnest call.
I am God.

'Be still and know that I am God,'
When aching burdens crush thy heart,
Then know I form thee for thy part
And purpose in the plan I hold.
Trust in God.

'Be still and know that I am God,'
Who made the atom's tiny span
And set it moving to My plan,
That I who guide the stars above
Will guide and keep thee in My love.
Be thou still.

Doran

Holiness doesn't mean doing extraordinary things, but doing ordinary things with love and faith.

Pope Francis

When I'm trying something new

A prayer for greater courage.

Lord,

The temptation to remain in my comfort zone can be very persuasive. It is easy to belittle my capabilities and make excuses before I have even begun. As I embark on this new endeavour, sustain me in my determination to stretch myself beyond what seems familiar and comfortable. In return, I will seek to use my gifts and talents to serve you more each day.

Amen

When I feel overwhelmed

*The best use of time when feeling overwhelmed
is to spend two minutes in quiet prayer; this
is far superior to ten minutes of panicking
about the length of your to-do list.*

Teach us, good Lord,
To serve Thee as Thou deservest;
To give, and not to count the cost;
To fight, and not to heed the wounds;
To toil, and not to seek for rest;
To labour, and not to ask for any reward save that
of knowing that we do Thy will.
Amen

St Ignatius of Loyola (1491–1556)

Watching the news

When watching or reading the news it is easy to feel despair and helplessness. In these moments, it can seem that prayer is all that we have.

Creator God,

As I look at events taking place around your world, I am often lost for words. In scenes of conflict and violence, I struggle to fathom the actions of humans. As I see the destruction caused by acts of nature, I wonder what purpose there can be in such suffering. At these moments, Lord, I choose to offer you my prayers rather than my questions.

Amen

A single grateful thought towards heaven is the most complete prayer.

Doris Lessing

When I go to sleep

*Concluding the day with a short time of
prayer can aid a restful sleep as well as develop
a greater sense of gratitude. You can craft your
own night prayer by adding your thoughts to
the end of each of these intentions.*

As this day ends, Lord,
    I thank you for these three simple moments of joy...
    I ask for your help with this challenging moment...
    I seek your pardon for...
    I hand over to your loving care...
    Amen

THE EARLY
YEARS

Starting school

Watching a child start school can often be more daunting for the parent than the child! A prayer together in the morning may ease any nerves.

Dear God,

Today I am going to school for the first time and it might feel a bit strange saying goodbye to my parents at the school gate. I know that I will enjoy making new friends and learning new things. Help me to remember that you will be with us and will watch over us as we play and learn, until home time.

Amen

Getting to know a new baby brother or sister

Whilst a new baby brings great joy, it can also be difficult for children to adapt to sharing the attention of their parents. This simple prayer for the older sibling focuses on this challenge.

Dear God,

I thank you for bringing .... into our family; I already know that I'm going to love them very much. Help me to be understanding when my mum and dad are busy caring for the new baby.

I also ask you to give me patience and encourage me to be a helpful big brother/sister and to not feel jealous or left out.

Amen

Going to a sleepover

*Early opportunities for independence can stir both
excitement and trepidation in children.*

Dear God,

Tonight I'm going to a sleepover and I won't be
staying at home. I'm very excited to be spending
time with my friends but I'm also worried about being
away from my family. I think that they might be a bit
worried as well. Be with us during this night; comfort
me if I'm feeling lonely and help me to enjoy this
exciting experience.

Amen

Be yourself; everyone else is already taken.

Oscar Wilde

Making friends

The gift of friendship is a treasure at any age.

Dear God,

Thank you for the gift of friendship. Help me to be nice to my friends and not to fight with them about silly things. I know that you will help me to choose good friends who will encourage me and make me feel good about myself. Thank you for sending my friends to me!

Amen

Becoming a teenager

Mark Twain famously wrote at age 21 that he was astonished at how much his father had learned in the seven years since he was 14.

Dear God,

Everything is changing around me and it's easy to be confused about whether I'm an adult now or not. Help me to remember that all I ever have to be is what you have made me. In the weeks, months and years ahead I will have to make lots of important decisions; help me to remember you in all of them.

Amen

Preparing for exams

Revision is always advised, but young people who find exam preparation bewildering might benefit from this prayer as a reminder of the end goal.

Lord,

I ask you to watch over me as I prepare for my exams. It can be easy to get downhearted when the hours of studying seem long and frustrating. Help me to remember my goal in trying to build a good life for myself, and I ask that with your guiding hand I may remain calm during each exam.

Amen

Every man's life is a fairy tale written by God's fingers.

Hans Christian Andersen

Dealing with gossip

*Whilst social media and the challenges it can
bring to young people are a recent development
in communication, gossip is certainly not. This
reflection was written in the mid-nineteenth century.*

Three Gates of Gold

If you are tempted to reveal
A tale to you someone has told
About another, make it pass,
Before you speak, three gates of gold.
These narrow gates: First, 'is it true?'
Then, 'is it needful?' In your mind
Give truthful answer. And the next
Is last and narrowest, 'Is it kind?'
And if to reach your lips at last
It passes through these gateways three,
Then you may tell the tale, nor fear
What the result of speech may be.

Beth Day

Arguing with parents

This prayer recognises that the transition to young adulthood can be difficult for everyone in a family.

Lord,

I'm in need of your grace at this moment. Sometimes the things my parents say make me feel angry and frustrated, especially when I express my need to step out as an adult on my own two feet. When we argue, it seems impossible to believe that they were ever young or that they have any faith in me. Be with us, as we travel through these challenging times together and remind us all of the power of admitting our mistakes and acknowledging how we feel.

Amen

Making good choices

Having all of the answers may be something
expected of parents, but it is seldom a possibility.
For young people struggling to make the right choice,
this reflection from St Paul may help.

Let your gentleness be known to everyone... Do not worry about anything, but in everything, by prayer and supplication with thanksgiving, let your requests be made known to God. And the peace of God, which surpasses all understanding, will guard your hearts and your minds in Christ Jesus.

Finally, beloved, whatever is true, whatever is honourable, whatever is just, whatever is pure, whatever is pleasing, whatever is commendable, if there is any excellence and if there is anything worthy of praise, think about these things... and the God of peace will be with you.

Philippians 4:5–9

Joy is not in things,
it is in us.

Charles Wagner

Living more simply

A prayer to help to remember
what is really important.

Lord,

There seems to be a big difference between the way the world expects me to live and the values that my faith has taught me. It is so easy to believe a person's value is defined by their possessions and to feel the pressure to conform. When I am faced with a difficult choice, help me to call to mind the values of my faith.

Amen

Accepting responsibility

*Acknowledging our vulnerabilities
and imperfections requires great courage.*

Today, Lord,

I got it wrong. Sometimes even more difficult than making a mistake is choosing to put it right. Help me to remember that I am not the choices I make, I am so much more than just the things that I do. Remind me of your love for me and the importance of owning my mistakes as opportunities for me to grow.

Amen

Leaving home

Moving out of the childhood home can seem such a daunting step; this prayer seeks company for the journey.

Lord,

The last box is packed and I'm leaving my family home to begin my life as an adult. I know there will be many changes to get used to and I am excited about a future filled with new experiences and events to learn from. Walk with me, Lord, as I begin this journey and help me to take with me the values and graces that my childhood has blessed me with.

Amen

MATTERS OF THE HEART

A prayer for love

This simple prayer serves as a reminder of the fundamental importance of love in our lives.

Where love is
There riches be.
Keep us all
From poverty.

Medieval prayer

First love

*Nothing should temper the joy
and excitement of first love.*

Lord,

   I am finding it impossible to concentrate on anything these days. My mind and heart are filled with thoughts and dreams of time spent with this special person. I am swept up with joy at the thought of them and I thank you for bringing them into my life. As we learn more about each other every day, may we grow closer together in trust, respect and understanding.

   Amen

Lonely at Valentine's

The commercial side of Valentine's Day can be particularly difficult for those not in a relationship.

Loving God,

Everywhere I look it seems I am surrounded by hearts and flowers and other symbols of romantic love. It is difficult, Lord, to be alone at this time which celebrates the joy of being in a loving relationship with another. I thank you for the many ways that I experience love with my family and friends; guide me to a greater understanding of the value of time spent alone and with those most important to me.

Amen

If you love until it hurts,
there can be no more hurt,
only more love.

Mother Teresa

Love is service of others

*St Francis of Assisi identifies in this prayer from
the thirteenth century the importance of putting
those that we love before ourselves.*

Oh Master, may I seek not so much to be
comforted as to comfort,
To be understood as to show understanding,
To be loved as to love;
For it is in giving that we receive,
In forgiving that we will be forgiven,
In dying that we shall rise up to life eternal.
Amen

St Francis of Assisi (*c.*1181–1226)

Unrequited love

*To recognise that your feelings for another person
are not reciprocated can be just as difficult as a
relationship coming to an end.*

It is painful, Lord,

To acknowledge that the overwhelming love that
I feel is not returned. To know that my efforts and
energy are in vain causes me great hurt. I need your
help, Lord, to let go of this love and to remain confident
in my own value and worth, trusting that you have a
greater plan for me.

Amen

Making a commitment

*A prayer in recognition of a
relationship moving forward.*

Lord,

I know we have reached an important moment in our relationship and I seek your blessing as we move forward together in commitment to one another. It can be frightening to acknowledge how much we need another person; guide us as we grow closer together and help us to trust our hearts to guide us.

Amen

One grain of love is better than a hundredweight of intellect.

Edward Bouverie Pusey

Before a proposal

*To ask for the hand of another in marriage
requires remarkable courage.*

I place into your loving care God,

The enormity of the task that lies ahead. As I prepare to make this proposal of marriage I ask for your guidance and blessing; may I find the right words at the right moment and be open to whatever answer I receive.

Amen

Healing a broken heart

*Whether a mutual decision or not, the end
of a relationship requires time to heal.*

Lord,

I know that loving another involves the risk of
heartache and today, I am hurting. The comforting
words of others are not easing my sadness and anger
and I feel lost as I find myself single again. Guide me,
Lord, to show myself compassion and patience as I
heal from this difficult time and when I am ready may
I seek the company of those who know me and love
me as I am.

Amen

Staying true to yourself

*The desire to be everything for someone
in a relationship can easily lead to losing a
sense of our individuality if we are not mindful
of our own self-worth.*

Creator God,

You have made me a special part of your creation, with a uniqueness and worth that at times I forget. In the excitement and passion of a new relationship, keep me steadfast to my true self and remind me of the important balance between wanting to please someone else and losing myself.

Amen

**You have to keep breaking
your heart until it opens.**

Rumi

The night before a wedding

*Amid the excitement and last-minute preparations,
a moment of reflection can bring calm to a
nervous bride or groom.*

Look with favour, O Lord,

Upon us as we begin our married life tomorrow.
Should we feel burdened with worry or nerves, may we
feel the love and support of those gathered together to
celebrate our commitment. In the years that lie ahead
of us, may we remember our wedding day with great
fondness and delight.

Amen

At the start of married life

*Preparing for a wedding and preparing for a
marriage are two very different things!
Once the confetti settles, the rich beauty
and mystery of a life together begins.*

God of love,

As we begin our life long journey together as a
married couple, we ask your blessing that the words
of our vows will remain instilled in our hearts in the
years that we look forward to together. Help us to
remember the importance of honesty, understanding
and faith in one another and in you.

Amen

Seasoned love

The remarkable commitment of many couples
married for decades serves as an inspiration
to those at the start of this journey.

Lord,

We have grown together like two vines, our roots entwined and our branches so interwoven that where one ends and the other begins is hard to see at times. Our story has been rich and varied and both our tears and laughter have helped us to grow together. We thank you for this wonderful gift and ask that you continue to bless us with patience and compassion and an unfailing resolve to never take the other for granted.

Amen

PARENTING AND FAMILY LIFE

Seeking pregnancy

A prayer for those at the start of the journey towards becoming a family.

Lord,

Look upon us with your favour as we embark on this journey together towards parenthood, knowing that all things are possible with faith and trust in you. As we wait patiently, may we grow closer together as a couple, building a solid foundation of love and understanding upon which our family can grow.

Amen

Struggling to conceive

A prayer for those who are waiting and hoping for a pregnancy.

Creator God,

I am in need of your loving care, as I struggle to keep the hope of parenthood alive. I always imagined that becoming a parent was part of my life plan and it feels as though my life is on hold at the moment. It can be difficult to be patient and to think of anything else at times. Be with me, Lord, as I strive to trust in your plan for my life.

Amen

Becoming pregnant

The moment of discovery of a pregnancy is often filled with an indescribable rush of emotions.

God of all creation,

We place into your hands this wondrous news; a new life is at its very beginning and we ask your blessing upon our son or daughter. We are filled with excitement and fear and longing and seek patience and strength for the months that lie ahead. As we make preparations in our home for our growing family, we ask your help in preparing our hearts and minds for the remarkable gift that is becoming parents.

Amen

For it was you who
formed my inward parts;
you knit me together in
my mother's womb.
I praise you, for
I am fearfully and
wonderfully made.

Psalm 139:13–14

On the birth of a baby

*A simple prayer to recognise the overwhelming
joy of meeting your child for the first time.*

I am filled with a joy, Lord,

That I could never have imagined possible. As I
gaze upon this beautiful miracle that has joined our
family I am overwhelmed with love and humbled by
this extraordinary gift. In the days and weeks that lie
ahead, bring us healing, rest and peace and watch
over and protect us as we grow together as a family.

Amen

Trusting yourself as a parent

*Well-intentioned or otherwise, parenting advice
seems to be everywhere and it is important
not to lose sight of our own innate sense of
what is right for our children.*

Lord,

I am surrounded by well-meaning advice on how
best to be a parent; friends and family and experts on
television seem to know what I should or shouldn't be
doing, more than I. You have granted me the precious
gift of becoming a parent; help me to trust my instincts
and what I know to be best for my children. For the
times I am struggling, grant me the humility to ask for
help from those whom I most trust.

Amen

A prayer of thanksgiving for parenting

Make time each day for a short prayer of thanksgiving for the many varied joys of parenthood.

I thank you, Lord,
For the joy of each new day as a parent
For the crayon drawings that adorn our fridge
For the consoling embraces
For the gift of making it better
For the excitement of every holiday
For the joyful greeting when I return home from work
For the soakings at bath time
For the wonder of watching my children sleeping
For the simple forgiveness when I get it wrong.
Amen

Remember, God does not pay us for results, but for effort.

St John Bosco

Feeling out of control

*As a parent, it can be a challenge to live in the
present moment and not become overwhelmed
by worry about the future.*

God of compassion,

I am struggling today with the enormous
responsibility of parenting. I find myself worrying
about so many things, many of which I have no hope
of controlling. Help me in these difficult moments to
remember the words of Julian of Norwich:

All shall be well, and all shall be well and
all manner of thing shall be well.

Draw me gently back to these words, Lord, when I find
myself lost in worry.

Amen

Moving house

The stress and excitement of moving house can also bring sadness as one chapter of family life comes to an end.

Lord,

As we say goodbye to our old house and move to a new home, we ask your blessing on our family at this exciting time. We thank you for all of the wonderful memories that we shared in our home and, with trust in you, we look forward to all of the good times that we will share as a family in our new home. Please bless it as a place filled with love and laughter.

Amen

For family holidays

*Wherever the destination, time together as a family
can be restorative for both body and soul.*

Lord,

As we begin our family holiday together we ask for
your care and protection. Keep us safe as we travel
and grant us patience to appreciate the excitement of
our children. We ask that this time together may be an
opportunity to relax with one another and a chance to
grow closer together as a family. May the treasured
memories of this time restore us when we return to
our hectic lives at home.

Amen

**The greatest prayer
is patience.**

Buddha

Death of a pet

*For many children, the death of a family pet can be
their first encounter with loss.*

Comfort us, O God,

In our sadness today as we say goodbye to our
treasured family pet. We thank you for the joy and
happiness that they brought to us. Although we find
it hard to accept that they have died, we hold onto the
many wonderful memories that they gave us.

Amen

For families at Christmas

This prayer is a reminder about what really matters at Christmas time as we try to steer away from the commercial hysteria that can surround the holiday.

God,

In the joy and excitement of decorating our home, the clamour to purchase last minute gifts and the relentless preparation of meals, help us to remember that to be part of a family at Christmas is to see its true meaning. Keep us patient with one another and may we never cease to be grateful for the many blessings we receive this and each day of the year.

Amen

Seeking forgiveness

If we want our children to recognise that it's OK to make mistakes, we need to have the courage to show them how it's done.

Lord,

I got it wrong today; it wasn't the first time and I'm sure it won't be the last. It takes courage as a parent to acknowledge our imperfections and poor choices. Help me to show my children the power of seeking and accepting forgiveness from one another. Remind me that regardless of the challenge or cost, your unfailing gift of forgiveness is one to be shared.

Amen

Forgiveness is not an occasional act, it is a constant attitude.

Martin Luther King Jr

When I have lost my keys

Traditionally, a prayer to St Anthony is invoked when a person seeks a lost but treasured possession. The following is an extract of one of many traditional prayers offered in such a crisis. On finding your lost item, it is also traditional to make a donation to the poor in gratitude to St Anthony for his help.

St Anthony, perfect imitator of Jesus,

Who received from God the special power of restoring lost things, grant that I may find.................. which has been lost. At least restore to me peace and tranquillity of mind, the loss of which has afflicted me even more than my material loss.

Amen

FOR OUR WORLD IN NEED

For those living in poverty

All of us can make small changes in our lives to tackle poverty both locally and globally.

Loving God,

I ask for your protection and care for all of those living in poverty both locally and throughout the world. I recognise that prayer alone will not eliminate poverty and ask for your help as I strive to lead a less selfish life; make me more generous with my time and resources to support those in need.

Amen

For peace in our world

Living a peaceful life is a step towards a peaceful world. What else can we offer? This simple Buddhist meditation seeks to calm the anxious and remind us of the role we play as peacemakers and peacekeepers.

I am Peace,
surrounded by Peace,
secure in Peace.
Peace protects me.
Peace supports me.
Peace is in me.
Peace is mine – All is well.
Peace to all beings,
Peace among all beings,
Peace from all beings.
I am steeped in Peace,
Absorbed in Peace.
In the streets, at our work,
having peaceful thoughts,
Peaceful words, peaceful acts.

Buddhist meditation

For those who are ill

This ancient Christian prayer asks for God's comfort
and protection, especially at night time.

Watch thou, dear Lord,
with those who wake, or watch, or weep tonight,
and give thine angels charge over those who sleep.
Tend thy sick ones, Lord Christ.
Rest thy weary ones.
Bless thy dying ones.
Soothe thy suffering ones.
Pity thine afflicted ones.
Shield thy joyous ones.
And all, for thy love's sake.
Amen.

St Augustine of Hippo (354–430 AD)

For world leaders

The need for compassion transcends
all political and geographical boundaries.

I pray today, Lord,

For the men and women who lead the nations of our world. Grant them wisdom and understanding and a compassion for all of humanity. May they recognise the humility their office requires and above all may they value human dignity and peace over power and wealth.

Amen

And what does the
Lord require of you
but to do justice, and
to love kindness, and
to walk humbly with
your God?

Micah 6:8

For the environment

It can be easy to take natural resources for granted and it can also be easy to make small changes to protect the environment.

Creator God,

We are surrounded by great beauty in the natural world which you have placed into our care and upon which our selfish actions have taken their toll. We ask that we may develop a greater respect for our world in order that it may be enjoyed by many generations to come.

Amen

For victims of natural disasters

Our faith can be shaken by the suffering of those affected by acts of nature.

God of compassion,

It seems unfair that it is often those communities struggling most with poverty and a lack of resources that are also affected most by natural disasters. At this time, I place into your loving care all of those whose lives have been lost and their grieving families. May I be generous in my support and prayer for those who work to bring aid to those most in need.

Amen

For greater religious tolerance

*The common ground between religions is
far greater than that which divides them.*

It seems easy, Lord,

To blame religion for the conflicts in our world and yet so many of the faiths of our world teach the importance of loving thy neighbour and treating others as we wish to be treated. The differences between different religious traditions may be complex, but to show respect and acceptance of the beliefs of others is simple; grant us this compassion and understanding, Lord.

Amen

Our prayer and God's mercy are like two buckets in a well; while one ascends, the other descends.

Bishop John Henry Hopkins

For victims of violence

*To be able to recognise that each human life is
a gift from God is to make a commitment to
non-violence and to seek peace for all people.*

Lord,

I pray today for all men, women and children who
are victims of violence. Every person is made in your
image and likeness and their life is a gift from you to
the world. Bring healing to all who suffer both in body
and mind and watch over those who work for justice
and peace.

Amen

For unsung heroes and heroines

The world is a kinder place than we might often perceive it to be; we have a duty to share news of the kindness of strangers.

Lord,

When I look at the news, sometimes it seems that only the tragedies of this world gain any media attention. I pray today for the men and women of our world who show great courage and bravery in the face of danger; those who risk their lives to protect strangers without a second thought for their own safety. When I read those news stories, I am reminded of your constant presence in our world.

Amen

TACKLING TEMPTATION

Sticking to a resolution

A resolution is a big step in the direction
towards the change you want to see in your life.

I am in need today, Lord,

As I commit to my resolution I acknowledge
the challenge of leaving my old ways behind and
embracing a healthier lifestyle. In moments of
temptation, Lord, remind me in the quiet of my heart
that I am capable of great inner strength with you
beside me.

Amen

Being honest

We are all human and we all get things wrong, and yet it can be so hard to acknowledge our imperfections to ourselves and others.

Faithful God,

I look to you for wisdom and courage today as I face my difficulty with acknowledging the truth. Help me when I struggle to admit my failings, remembering that you love me just as I am. As I strive to make the right choices may I always keep in mind that I am not defined by the mistakes that I make, but by my efforts to make amends.

Amen

Giving up a bad habit

*This prayer acknowledges that sometimes we need
more than willpower and good intentions.*

Lord,

I am making the first step today to becoming
the best person that I can. Whilst I am fired with
enthusiasm in this present moment, I recognise that
the journey ahead will be filled with moments of
weakness and self-doubt. In these moments may I
know your love in my heart and recognise it in the kind
words and actions of those around me.

Amen

My business is not
to remake myself,
But to make the absolute
best of what God made.

Robert Browning

For those who suffer with an addiction

A prayer for compassion and strength for those who need it most.

Loving God,

Look with favour today on those suffering with an addiction and their family and friends. You alone have the power to make all things new as you shower us with unlimited love and compassion. May those battling to overcome addiction know that you walk alongside us, waiting without judgement to support us through the challenge of each new day.

Amen

For determination in difficult situations

*This prayer was written a century ago by a
renowned Bengali poet, artist and thinker who
received the Nobel Prize in Literature in 1913.*

Let me not pray to be sheltered from dangers
but to be fearless in facing them.
Let me not beg for the stilling of my pain
but for the heart to conquer it.
Let me not look for allies in life's battlefield
but to my own strength.
Let me not crave in anxious fear to be saved
but hope for the patience to win my freedom.
Grant me that I may not be a coward, feeling
your mercy in my success alone;
but let me find the grasp of your hand in my failure.

Rabindranath Tagore (1861–1941)

For help in thinking before acting

Our first response is not always the most appropriate in times of stress or provocation. This 2,500-year-old prayer reminds us of the simple need to think first.

O God,
Grant that no word may fall from us,
Against our will,
Unfit for the present need.
Amen

Pericles (495–429 BC)

A noble deed is a
step towards God.

Josiah Gilbert Holland

Fighting fair

Disagreements are a healthy part of any relationship; the challenge is focusing on the issue and not the person involved.

God,

There are times when I know the quickest way to end a conflict is to hurt the other person with a past mistake or character trait that they struggle with. I need to remember the importance of responding calmly whilst considering the other person's point of view. Help me to keep in mind my own imperfections and focus on the problem at hand without judgement of others.

Amen

Communicating with clarity

A human voice and a human face make any communication easier to understand and respond to, even if it does require bravery at times.

Lord,

I ask for your help today for courage to communicate with others honestly and with compassion. It is tempting at times to fire off an email or message rather than face a difficult conversation in person or on the telephone. May my interactions with others, no matter how challenging they might feel, leave both parties at ease.

Amen

To reach the port of Heaven we must sail sometimes with the wind and sometimes against it. But we must sail, and not drift nor lie at anchor.

Oliver Wendell Holmes Sr

CARING
FOR MIND
AND BODY

Being more grateful

With daily practice, the attitude of gratitude
can become a healthy habit.

Lord,

   Each day of my life is filled with so many moments I am grateful for, and yet I often rush through each day without giving them a second thought. Help me to slow down, take deeper breaths and see your beauty and grace in the simple blessings that each day brings.

   Amen

Dealing with anger

*It's very normal to feel anger; the daily
challenge is deciding not to use our anger
as an excuse for hurting others.*

Compassionate God,

It is so hard to know what to do when I feel angry.
It's so easy sometimes to turn it on others, especially
those who are closest to me. I ask most of all for the
courage to acknowledge when I am feeling angry
knowing that it is a normal aspect of being human.
Encourage me to use my anger as a motivation to
make a positive change in my life.

Amen

Sharing joy with others

*Seek out opportunities to bring a moment
of joy to a stranger today.*

God,

As I grow better at recognising the good in my life,
help me to share that joy with others. A little gesture
of happiness shared with a stranger can have a
remarkable effect on the life of another. I know that
fixing many of the ills of this world is beyond my
limited capabilities, help me always to remember the
small ways I can make a difference.

Amen

Joy runs deeper than despair.

Corrie ten Boom

Visiting hospital

*Whatever the reason, a visit to hospital can
be a worrying time; a moment of calm prayer
can allay any fears.*

Lord,

As I prepare to visit the hospital today I ask your blessing upon myself and all who are in need of healing, whether in body or mind. For those who are staying in hospital, be with them in the quiet moments of the day if they struggle with fear and loneliness. I thank you for the compassion of those who work in healthcare; guide their hands and hearts today.

Amen

When a child is ill

It can be so difficult to know what to do when a child is sick; many families draw comfort from the knowledge that they are being remembered in prayer.

Healing God,

I feel helpless before you as I think of this young person who is struggling with poor health. What can I offer but my love and prayers; what do I have but my faith in you? I pray for their healing and ask you to be with all of us. Bring comfort to family and friends and kindness and wisdom to all those who care for the sick. I ask this knowing that nothing is impossible to you.

Amen

Waiting for test results

*It can feel impossible to look to the future when
awaiting important medical test results. Seek
comfort from the words of St Francis de Sales.
Reflect on these words and their importance
for you as you pray today.*

Do not look forward in fear to the changes of life;
rather look to them with full hope that as they arise,
God, whose very own you are,
will lead you safely through all things;
and when you cannot stand it,
God will carry you in His arms.
Do not fear what may happen tomorrow;
the same everlasting Father who cares for you today
will take care of you today and every day.
He will either shield you from suffering,
or will give you unfailing strength to bear it.
Be at peace,
and put aside all anxious thoughts and imaginations.

St Francis de Sales (1567–1622)

**Oft hope is born,
when all is forlorn.**

J. R. R. Tolkien

Getting the 'all clear'

A prayer of thanksgiving for a clean bill of health.

Lord,

I have carried such fear and worry with me in recent weeks, and today I feel such a sense of joy and relief at the good news. It feels as though I have been given a second chance and I have a duty to make the most of each precious day. Help me to remember this feeling and guide me to find the best purpose for my life. I ask today, for your blessing on my health and all those awaiting important test results.

Amen

Dealing with depression

Holding steadfast to faith in God during depression can be a challenge, but also a source of great comfort. This prayer was found in St Teresa of Ávila's prayer book upon her death.

Let nothing disturb thee,
Nothing affright thee
All things are passing;
God never changeth;
Patient endurance
Attaineth to all things;
Who God possesseth
In nothing is wanting;
Alone God sufficeth.

St Teresa of Ávila (1515–1582)

There are many
things that can only
be seen through eyes
that have cried.

Óscar Romero

Feeling hatred

We strive each day to live with love for our neighbour and all whom we meet; this is surely the greatest challenge that each human faces. This prayer comes from the Talmud, a collection of Jewish law from the fourth and fifth century AD.

May it be thy will, O Lord,

That no man foster hatred against us in his heart, and that we foster no hatred in our hearts against any man; that no man foster envy of us in his heart, and that we foster not envy in our hearts of any man.

Amen

The Talmud

PROVIDING

Looking for a new job

A prayer for those seeking employment.

God of hope,

Walk with me on this journey as I search to find a new job that will help me to provide for my family and fill me with a sense of purpose in my life. Guide me, Lord, towards a job that will allow me to support myself and those who need me, and that will satisfy me and use my skills well.

Amen

Before a job interview

It can be worrying to know you have a limited time to show the best of yourself to a potential employer and this prayer aims to provide you with reassurance.

Loving God,

I ask for your help as I prepare for this job interview. Fill me with a sense of your peace and calm and guide me as I try to show the very best of myself to those interviewing me. In moments of self-doubt, may I remember my strengths and that all things that happen are part of your plan for my life. Lord, I place all of my trust in you.

Amen

For money worries

This prayer offers support to those who are experiencing financial difficulties.

Lord,

I come to you in need as I struggle to provide for myself and my family. It is easy to feel blame for the situation I find myself in. I know that there are many riches in my life, but I am frightened for the future and can't see how to straighten things out. Grant me the courage to seek help and support knowing that you walk with us in the darkest days.

Amen

All I can 'pay back' to God or others or myself is who I really am.

Richard Rohr

For ethical spending

A prayer for greater awareness of fair trade issues.

Lord,

There is such pressure to keep up with others who surround themselves with materialistic possessions and it is easy to distance myself from the unethical practices experienced by many workers in the world, as I seek the cheapest version of the latest trend. May I remember the true value and worth of people rather than possessions.

Amen

Learning to say 'no' at work

We can only do so much with the hours that we spend at work; this prayer is for those who find it difficult to say 'no' to their colleagues.

Lord,

The tasks ahead seem impossible. As I try to manage so many things at once, guide me to find your peace in those pursuits that really matter. May I learn the value of saying 'no' and recognise the importance of dedicating my time and capabilities to that which best serves you and others.

Amen

Dealing with redundancy

Whatever our job entails, it can play a significant role in our sense of purpose and worth.

Lord,

I find myself out of work and it is difficult not to feel fearful for what lies ahead. I trust that you have a plan for my life, but in this moment I am not sure where I am heading. Guide my heart, Lord, to have the strength I need to persevere, and to stay hopeful about the future.

Amen

It is only through labour and prayerful effort, by grim energy and resolute courage, that we move on to better things.

Theodore Roosevelt

After a promotion

A prayer for those taking on a new role or
responsibility in the workplace.

God,

    I begin this day in a new role at work and I am excited about the opportunities that the future holds for me. I thank you for the skills that you have given to me and I ask for your help as I take on more responsibility. Guide me to make ethical choices and help me to model the principles of my faith in the workplace.

    Amen

For greater work–life balance

Do we live to work or work to live?

Gracious God,

Guide me with your spirit to find the right balance between time at work and time with my family. It can be so easy to get swept up in the demands of my job, that I find myself sacrificing time spent with the most important people in my life. In these moments, may I find the strength to put that which I treasure most, first.

Amen

For finding meaning at work

This reflection from the nineteenth century serves as a reminder of the importance of seeking work that we enjoy and that suits our God-given abilities.

From **Andrew Rykman's Prayer**
Make my mortal dreams come true
With the work I fain would do;
Clothe with life the weak intent,
Let me be the thing I meant;
Let me find in Thy employ
Peace that dearer is than joy;
Out of self to love be led
And to heaven acclimated,
Until all things sweet and good
Seem my natural habitude.

John Greenleaf Whittier (1807–1892)

Disturb us, Lord,
to dare more boldly,
To venture on wider seas
Where storms will show
your mastery;
Where losing sight of land,
We shall find the stars.

Sir Francis Drake

Being busy at work

Whilst it is unlikely we are facing the same challenges
in our work day as Sir Jacob Astley faced when he
wrote this before the battle of Edgehill in 1642, we
can all relate to the sentiment.

Lord,
Thou knowest how busy we must be this day.
If we forget thee, do not thou forget us.
Amen

Sir Jacob Astley (1579–1652)

THE
GOLDEN
YEARS

For retirement

A prayer for the transition into life after work.

Ever-loving God,

I am embarking on a new stage in my life as I begin my retirement; this precious time that I have sought so fiercely in recent years. Be with me in these first days and weeks as I adjust to having time for myself and my family. Help me to find a peaceful balance between rest and activity, recognising that rather than being an end, this is an exciting beginning.

Amen

On becoming a grandparent

*A prayer of thanksgiving to welcome
a new generation.*

Oh what joy it is Lord,

To welcome into the world a new child. As I begin
on this journey as a grandparent, I thank you for this
wonderful grandchild. I ask your blessing upon this
new family; as we learn to embrace our new roles may
we be generous with our time, patience and experience.

Amen

Moving house

It can be difficult to say goodbye to a home, especially if the move into a new one is out of necessity. Take a moment to acknowledge the joys of the past and the present moment of sadness.

Lord,

Today I close the door on our family home and begin another chapter of my life in a new house. It seems strange to say goodbye to a building as though it were an additional member of our family, but it holds such treasured memories which I carry with me to this new living space. Comfort me through any sadness as I look forward to the new memories that lie ahead.

Amen

Losing a partner

A prayer for the most difficult of days.

Heavenly God,

I am lost for words at the moment as I try to grasp the space left behind by my closest friend and love. I am surrounded by the loving support of family and friends and yet I feel overwhelmed. Walk with me through these dark days as I hold onto these comforting words from the New Testament:

He will wipe every tear from their eyes.
Death will be no more;
mourning and crying and pain will be no more,
for the first things have passed away.

Amen

Receiving a bus pass

The attitude with which the pensioner's bus pass is received seems telling of a person's approach to embracing ageing with a little humour.

Lord,

I'm trying to see the humour in it; an envelope dropped onto the mat today and within it was my pensioner's bus pass. I'm wondering how it's possible that it bears my name and photograph, I can't quite believe that I have reached the age that this occasion suggests. Grant me the humility to acknowledge the rich wisdom of my life experience and the courage to look ahead to the many adventures still to come.

Amen

For feeling regret

It is inevitable that at times we feel regret.
We are the person God made us to be and
we must remember that we are more than
the good and bad choices we have made in life.

All that we ought to have thought, and not thought,
All that we ought to have said and have not said,
All that we ought to have done and have not done;
All that we ought not to have spoken
and yet have spoken,
All that we ought not to have done and yet have done;
For thoughts, words, and works pray we,
O Lord, for forgiveness,
And repent with penitence.
Amen

Zoroaster (*c.*628–*c.*551 BC)

Four things come not back:
The spoken word;
The sped arrow;
Time past;
The neglected opportunity.

-
Umar Ibn Al-Khattab,
the second caliph

For accepting help

*Making the adjustment to needing assistance
can bring frustration and sadness; this prayer
asks for gracious understanding.*

God,

I thank you that you have granted me a lifetime of
joy and happiness. I have been blessed with good
health and strength of mind and so it is difficult for
me to admit that I need the support of others. Help me
to remember that this support is a gift that enhances
my life rather than being a hindrance; keep pride and
stubbornness from my heart and in difficult moments
replace them with gratitude for the kindness of others.

Amen

Dealing with illness

*The psychological difficulties associated
with a lengthy illness can often remain once
the time of physical symptoms have passed.
The following extract from the book of Job in
the Old Testament serves as a reminder
that the difficult days will soon pass.*

You will forget your misery;
you will remember it as waters
that have passed away.
And your life will be brighter than the noonday;
its darkness will be like the morning.
And you will have confidence, because there is hope;
you will be protected and take your rest in safety.

Job 11:16–18

Recognising wisdom
and experience

*A prayer for greater recognition of all that
can be learnt from the older generation.*

Lord,

It seems that everyone is in a rush these days.
Wherever I turn, people are immersed in so many
distractions, I cannot keep up and I'm not sure that I
want to! It can feel as though the world moves quickly
on and the wisdom and experience of our generation
is overlooked. Open the eyes of society to recognise
the valuable contribution that we have to make.

Amen

Prayer is nothing else than being on terms of friendship with God.

St Teresa of Ávila

Seeking God's grace and support each day

This simple daily prayer reminds us of our trust in God's presence in our lives each day.

May he support us all the day long till the shades lengthen and the evening comes and the busy world is hushed and the fever of life is over and our work is done. Then in his mercy may he give us a safe lodging and a holy rest and peace at the last.

Amen

Blessed John Henry Newman (1801–1890)

SEEKING ANSWERS TO THE BIG QUESTIONS

Why am I here?

Lord,

It seems so strange to me that we do not choose to be born and usually do not choose to die. Is our life on earth just a random act? I know how I was born, but to ponder the reason why I was born seems impossible. Fill me with your Spirit, Lord, as I seek the purpose of my life.

Amen

What does the future hold?

Therefore I tell you, do not worry about your life, what you will eat or what you will drink, or about your body, what you will wear. Is not life more than food and the body more than clothing? Look at the birds of the air; they neither sow nor reap nor gather into barns, and yet your heavenly Father feeds them. Are you not of more value than they? And can any of you by worrying add a single hour to your span of life?... So do not worry about tomorrow, for tomorrow will bring worries of its own. Today's trouble is enough for today.

Matthew 6:25–27 and 34

Doubt isn't the opposite of faith; it is an element of faith.

Paul Tillich

Is there a plan for my life?

Eternal God,

Too often I rush through each day and each week, looking ahead and wondering if there is a plan for my life. It can be challenging to live in the present moment and to relish the simple joys of life rather than worrying about what direction my life might take. Remind me, Lord, that worrying about the future does nothing to change it.

Amen

What happens when I die?

Lord of life,

When I think of my loved ones who have passed away, I draw comfort in the knowledge that my faith tells me that death is not the end. When I think of those who suffer, I have to believe that the promise of eternal life will be fulfilled. Strengthen my trust in this promise, especially when I find my own faith being challenged.

Amen

Surely goodness and mercy shall follow me all the days of my life, and I shall dwell in the house of the Lord my whole life long.

Psalm 23

Does God exist?

Lord,

I am a work in progress and on some days I seek but cannot find you. I thank you for the gift of a faith that questions and challenges me and for the many ways that you work in my life; often through the words and actions of others. When I wander far from you, you wait patiently for me, as a parent who trusts their child to make the right choice.

Amen

Which path am I meant to choose?

Lord,

   I am facing a difficult choice and I am reminded of Robert Frost's poem:

> Two roads diverged in a wood, and I–
> I took the one less travelled by,
> And that has made all the difference.

Sometimes there is an easy option but it is not always the right one. I ask with the help of your Spirit, that I might keep my faith in mind as I make this decision.

   Amen

When the solution is simple, God is answering.

Albert Einstein

Why are people cruel to one another?

Compassionate God,

I believe that you created us in your image and likeness and my faith in your love for us is unwavering. But I struggle, God, with the suffering I see in the world; how can humans treat one another with such hatred and place such little value on human life? How can you bear it? I pray today for all of those who are suffering and that your Spirit will work to heal the hearts of those who cause suffering to others.

Amen

PRAYING THROUGH THE YEAR

For the New Year

A prayer for new beginnings.

Lord,

As I begin this New Year, I resolve to make the most of each day and opportunity that is presented to me. It is easy to claim a handful of unrealistic resolutions; I instead aim for the prayer of St Richard of Chichester:

> May we know you more clearly,
> love you more dearly,
> and follow you more nearly,
> day by day.

Amen

During the season of Lent

A prayer for renewed faith.

God,

As I begin this Lenten journey, I commit with your grace to a time of prayer, fasting and good works. May I remember to call on you in both times of need and gratitude. I resolve to live more simply, focusing on my needs rather than my desires and I pray for the courage to reach out to others in need.

Amen

On Mother's Day

A prayer of thanksgiving for mothers.

Gracious God,

I offer my prayer today for mothers throughout the world whose selfless comfort and care nourish the children of our world. As I thank you for the mothering figures in my own life and I place into your loving care those for whom Mother's Day brings sadness rather than joy, particularly those who are recently bereaved or separated from their families.

Amen

During the season of Easter

A prayer for the hope and joy that Easter celebrates.

The Hymn of Joy
Joyful, joyful, we adore Thee,
God of glory, Lord of love;
hearts unfold like flow'rs before Thee,
Opening to the Sun above,
Melt the clouds of sin and sadness;
drive the dark of doubt away;
Giver of immortal gladness,
fill us with the light of day!

All Thy works with joy surround Thee,
earth and heav'n reflect Thy rays,
stars and angels sing around Thee,
center of unbroken praise:
Field and forest, vale and mountain,
Flow'ry meadow, flashing sea,
chanting bird and flowing fountain,
call us to rejoice in Thee.

Henry Van Dyke (1852–1933)

On Father's Day

A prayer of thanksgiving for fathers.

Loving God,

Whom many call 'Father' I bring before you in prayer today fathers throughout the world, whose tenderness and strength provides a loving presence in the lives of children throughout the world. I thank you for the father figures in my life and seek your blessing upon those who find this day difficult; for children and fathers who are separated and for those recently bereaved.

Amen

At the start of the school year

A prayer for all of those in education.

God,

   As children and teachers prepare for the start of this new school year, I thank you for the remarkable gift of education and I pray that it is never taken for granted by the young people in my life. Bring patience and compassion to all those who work in education and I pray that education for all of the world's children will soon become a reality.

   Amen

On All Saints' Day

*A prayer for those who dedicate their lives
to the service of others.*

Lord,

As I remember those remarkable men and women of faith who put the service of others first in their lives, I ask that by their example I may seek to live more closely according to your plan for my life. May I never fail to recognise opportunities to follow the inspiration of the saints in my own life.

Amen

On Remembrance Day

A prayer to remember those who have died.

Lord,

In this month of November as we remember those who have died, and particularly those who have given their lives in the service of their country, help me be mindful of the value of peace and freedom. As I recall with love, cherished memories of those who have passed away, may I commit to making the most of each day of my life, honouring all of the ways in which it was enhanced by knowing them.

Amen

During the season of Advent

A prayer about waiting and anticipation.

God of light,

   We are eagerly awaiting the arrival of Christmas and it seems that each year the decorations and gift giving starts earlier and earlier. Help me God, to use this season of Advent as a chance to remember the importance of waiting and to seize this opportunity to reflect upon what is really important in my life and my faith.

   Amen

During the season
of Christmas

A prayer to celebrate light conquering darkness.

Lord,

The extraordinary story of the birth of Jesus is about the triumph of light over darkness; it reminds me of your active presence in our world. In the dark moments of my life and in the situations in our world where it seems darkness reigns, I pray today for your light and love to be known and shared. May this Christmas bring peace to all people throughout the world.

Amen